E-commerce

A beginners guide to E-commerce

Introduction

I want to thank you and congratulate you for downloading the book, *"Ecommerce"*.

This book has lots of actionable information on how to make money online with ecommerce.

The world is increasingly becoming tech driven. Think about it; you (or someone you know) have probably purchased something online. By so doing, you are probably among the over 40% of internet users (over 1 billion people) who have purchased something online via mobile, desktop, tablet or other devices. If you think about it from a business perspective, this means there is a huge potential to make money if you are a seller (1 billion potential customers!) and.

But how can you go about it? How can you get a share of the over a share of over US$1.2 trillion that's transacted online every single year?

Well, this book will show you exactly how to go about it. Whether you want to set up a C2C (customer to customer) business, a B2C (business to customer) business, or a B2B (business to business) business, it is important to build a solid understanding of the concept of ecommerce so that you start off with a strong understanding of the ins and outs of ecommerce. This book will show you everything you need to know about ecommerce to ensure you know what works, what doesn't and how to be the best at what you do.

Thanks again for downloading this book. I hope you enjoy it!

Table of Contents

Before we discuss the specifics of ecommerce, it is important to start by building a strong background of what it entails as well as how ecommerce businesses make money.

Understanding Ecommerce

What Is An Ecommerce Business?

Ecommerce businesses are those businesses that seek to transmit products, services, and naturally, funds online. They vary greatly in terms of size as well as scope. The size varies from retail giants like Alibaba, eBay, Etsy and Amazon to small websites that are run by individuals.

How do Ecommerce Businesses Make Money?

We will start at the very beginning- by explaining how ecommerce businesses/websites make money before moving on to show you how to start your own ecommerce business.

How do ecommerce sites make money? Well, the profit model here is simple; you sell products then make income out of it. The income here may be in the form of profits from products you have stocked or products you are dropshipping. At other times, you are paid a commission for every sale made through your referrals.

It may be clear on how you stand to make a profit by selling your own product (products you've stocked), but many people do not understand how you can make a profit by selling another person's product (dropshipping and affiliate commissions).

To help you understand, this part will be dedicated to showing you how you stand to make a profit from selling other people's products.

We will keep it as simple here as possible.

Here is how a typical ecommerce operates.

1. Get a good wholesaler. The wholesaler is the party that you will purchase the products in bulk from. You can probably see where this is going. Buying the product in bulk will then allow you to have massive discounts.

2. Advertise these products in your ecommerce store. Try to standardize your prices. It does not make much sense to have prices that are either too high or too low. Try to adhere to the prices that are present in the majority of sites that are selling that very product.

3. After the first two steps have been taken care of, promote the products you have on sale. Also, make sure to give your customers great deals to increase sale

4. As an added bonus, make sure you have a blog on your website that will be dedicated towards these products. Ensure the blog covers the importance of these products, how to use them, different creative ways of deriving the most value from such products and any

relevant information that can add value to the current and prospective customer. If you do this in a competent and consistent way, you will soon establish yourself as an authority in that field in the eyes of your customer base.

We will learn more about that later.

What if you do not have money and thus cannot afford to purchase products? What if you don't want to go through the hassle of dealing with inventory i.e. shipping, storage, etc. Well, if stocking products is not a viable option for you, do not worry; you have several other options:

- There are services, like ClickBank, that were created with ecommerce businesspeople in mind. Using these services, you can market other people's products then when you make a sale, you will be paid a commission (everything is automated). In this case, you will be an affiliate; you won't need to stock anything, develop any products or services. All you will need to do is to have an audience to whom you can recommend various products, which you are an affiliate. Other websites that allow affiliates include Amazon Associates, Shareasale.com, CJ (formerly Commission Junction) etc.

Note: The thing is; affiliate marketing is the easiest and most risk free option you can pursue perhaps because you don't have to stock anything to start. Moreover, it is the easiest to manage since you won't have to deal with customers (the product owner deals with that).

Now that you understand what ecommerce is as well as how you can make money from ecommerce, let's move on to learn the specifics of building an ecommerce business from home.

How To Get Started

Starting and launching an ecommerce business is not easy. It has never been easy, even in those early days when only a few people had an idea on how ecommerce worked. And yet, creating and launching sites that entrepreneurs, retailers, manufacturers, wholesalers, creators and designers can sell their products has never been more viable and attainable.

Depending on what business you are in, it may make a lot of sense to launch the ecommerce side of your business before you can consider the typical brick and mortar setting (remember some businesses don't require a B&M model e.g. selling domains, plugins, software, ebooks etc.).

However, you have to understand that there exist several key differences in how you approach building ecommerce websites as opposed to traditional businesses.

Before you get to working on humane elements: before you can start working on cultivating trust with your future clientele, you will have to lay the foundation.

Obviously, you cannot start anything without knowing what it is you are going to be selling. Therefore, naturally, the first thing you need to do is to decide what you want to sell.

Decide What To Sell

This is perhaps one of the most challenging steps probably because it influences very many things especially the business model, ease of automation, your level of involvement, costs involved, skills level and such. For instance, if you are going to opt to be selling digital products, the things you will need to deal with will be different from when you opt for a physical product. Whichever option you go for, your decision to choose a product could be influenced by your desire to fulfill any of the following 8 points:

Product Creation Opportunities

- ✓ Look for an opportunity gap: In this case, you will be developing a business to solve a problem for something that is missing in the market.

- ✓ Follow your passion: This simply entails developing a business based on your own passions e.g. photography, gardening, etc.; you can develop a business out of that.

- ✓ Capitalize on a trend: This is pretty straightforward; ride on trends and make successful products out of it e.g. selling branded t-shirts for Olympics for instance.

- ✓ Utilize your experience and expertise: With some expertise and experience, you will be much better placed to get started since you will already be an authority just trying to find your footing.

- ✓ Identify and cater to various consumer passions: In this type of business, you provide products that make the lives of people pursuing various passions or habits better e.g. sporting or camping gear.

✓ Identify and solve various customer pain points: In this case, you develop an ecommerce business that centers around solving certain problems that customers are actively looking for solutions to.

✓ Build a pretty interesting as well as captivating brand: This is a slow but long term approach to building a sustainable ecommerce business because it focuses on setting yourself apart from the competition.

✓ Uncover various opportunities in keywords: You leverage on your knowledge on the power of search engines and SEO to start a successful ecommerce business

Is It Sellable?

The different product creation opportunities are likely to bear a wide array of product types. For instance, you might come up with both digital and physical products. Whatever it is, the most important thing is to determine whether:

✓ There is a potential market for that; do your research. You can learn more about that here.

✓ The product is a viable one. You can learn how to determine the viability of your product idea here and here.

✓ You really want to sell that product and want to be associated with it

✓ You can commit to selling the product and dedicate a reasonable amount of time and other resources towards building the ecommerce business

Getting A Ready-To-Sell Product

Once you've settled on a product, it is now time to think of how you will get it for you to sell it. You have either of the following options:

✓ Make your own: Creating your product from scratch using various raw materials- you need to be an expert on whatever it is you want to create

✓ Manufacturer: Coming up with a product idea, then having a local or overseas manufacturer to make it for you

✓ Wholesale: Buying in bulk, getting a discount then selling at a profit

✓ Dropship: Selling stuff you don't stock by having another person/entity do the order fulfillment. All you need to do is to send the order details to the supplier who then ships the product to the customer. In simple terms, you never have to deal with the product. You can learn more about dropshipping here and here.

The model you opt for might be influenced by such factors as what you intent to sell for instance. The model you choose will influence such factors as the ease of making sales, profitability, scalability, your level of involvement and the likelihood of staying in business over the long term.

To find suppliers for your physical products if that's the business model you want to pursue, you can check this comprehensive guide on some of the top places to find suppliers.

Prepare A Business Plan

Without one, you are essentially setting yourself up to fail. You cannot possibly have everything figured out in your head! You need to have all your ideas put down in writing and organized nicely for you and anyone else keen to know about your business to look at it. You can learn the specifics of preparing a comprehensive business plan here.

Note: Throughout the rest of the book, 'products' in this book will be used to denote physical products. Of course, as I already stated, you can sell both digital and physical products online; we will use physical products for illustration purposes here.

Before moving to the next step, it is important to keep some things in mind:

Things You Must Look Out For When Starting Ecommerce Business

It is so very easy to view ecommerce as a simple, no-frills way you can make money, build assets and truly milk all that the internet's global reach has to offer.

What is the reality though? Well, the reality is that ecommerce is not nearly as easy. Sure enough, anybody may have a website that has stuff on sale but how do you go about convincing folk to show up on your site? How do you take care of logistics, especially if the supplier who provides the goods is several thousand miles away?

E-commerce stores have the potential to be a superb business to get into. However, this is only true if you do things the right way, and take the necessary time to teach yourself how to execute it well. If what you are looking for is a get rich quick scheme, you would be wise to head somewhere else.

This chapter is going to look at 3 things that you ought to really consider and be watchful of as you are starting out your ecommerce store.

1. "Niche Down"

You probably have an idea, or several of them. You are convinced that your ideas will absolutely smash everything else, given how unique you know them to be.

Well, let us clear something here: there are tens of millions of fellows looking to make a buck from the internet. After all, internet is the new real estate. Regardless of how unique you think your idea is, there are at least hundreds of other people with a similar idea looking to succeed off of it.

You need to "niche down", which basically means to be more specific with the service or product.

Take this example:

If you aim to sell cases for tablets and mobile phones, it seems like a good idea to throw everything you have at acquiring the biggest hold of iPhone and iPad covers this side of the sun, right? After all, Apple is still growing rapidly, is it not? You are wrong if you think this is a good idea. There are tens if not hundreds of thousands of fellows looking to sell off iPhone covers. The market is often so saturated you may well be committing financial suicide if you choose this route. A better idea would be to focus on Kindle Fire covers. Here, you are dealing with a new product that not many people have had a chance to explore. It is a lot easier to establish yourself as an authority in an environment that is not too saturated. The idea is to niche down until you can find a safe space in which you can operate in.

2. Test before Investing

Have you ever had a brilliant idea; an idea so brilliant that you were convinced you would change the world with it? Did you then follow up the conception of the idea with lots and lots of money spent developing it, only to find that the only ones that cared for it were your spouse and perhaps your kids? We have all been there at least once. The burn you get from the experience is potent enough to destroy your spirit.

Therefore, before you explode into action on your new site, test it "for congruence". What we mean here is that you should:

1. Test if your product or niche attracts interest

2. Test to see if your offer converts

So how do you go about this? The answer is easy and straightforward- start a blog. Let me explain this with an example:

Simon Stock, a surfboard rack company owner knew very little about surfboard racks. However, he was a smart fellow who was willing to learn. So he took an afternoon off and set up a simplistic WordPress blog that focused exclusively on surfboard racks. For several weeks, he took some time to write up on surfboard racks. He also made sure to include some Amazon affiliate links on the blog's side-bar that he pointed his readership to. Within no time, he began to see a steady bump up in organic traffic on his blog and he started to get affiliate sales on Amazon (remember I mentioned Amazon Associates as a way to make money without owning any product).

Simon Stock not only got to find out that there was a steady market for his product, but he learned infinitely more on surfboard racks than he had before. What Simon did here was test before thinking of expansion.

From there, he then setup his ecommerce site and built relationships with major manufacturing people. He used the test site as his lead funnel to his new site. Today, Simon Stock is one of the internet's biggest resellers of the surfboard rack.

3. Manufacturing in Asia Will Give You Several Migraines and Probably a Nasty Ulcer

For starters, why is this point here? We will answer this one with a question of our own- why is this point not emphasized in every ecommerce guide written? You know what the problem with many ecommerce fellows is? They overheard from a friend that Apple's assembly line is in China and after a quick search on Google, ascertained that this was valid. Then they read in Robert. T. Kiyosaki's book that his very first startup had its manufacturing base in Asia. So they immediately concluded that manufacturing in Asia is the way to go, as the pay rates are significantly lower.

Sourcing in Asia can be truly phenomenal. It is as cheap as cheap goes, and there are thousands of little companies set up to exclusively work on custom tailored products. There is also the fact that in Asia, you can make just about anything. Take this last statement as it is- if you are the edgy sort who likes to dabble in that grey area between potent supplements and illegal steroids, you will not have too much of a hard time finding some base in Asia that will be happy to work on your fantasy. That said, there are several problems with sourcing from Asia:

- ✓ Language barrier is a real problem, and you will be up against it at some point, inevitably.

- ✓ Quality control is a real nightmare.

- ✓ Asians tend to approach business, and the concepts of business in a way that is quite different from the average westerner's.

If you are serious on doing your manufacturing in Asia, then you should consider teaming up with someone whom you trust and who understands the local language. He must also be on the ground and is able to work closely with the factories regularly. This is to ensure that you are getting the exact product that you ordered.

If you are serious about doing business online, one very important step of laying your foundation is by taking care of the paperwork and ensuring that you are compliant with the necessary agencies, the same way that you would go about things if you were starting a business that had a physical bearing and location.

Working Through The Red Tape

There are several basic bureaucratic hoops that you have to jump through, en-route to launching your ecommerce business.

These include:

- Selecting and then registering your business name.

- Choosing and purchasing a domain name: You can purchase domain your domain name from GoDaddy, iPage, Hostgator, BlueHost and from various other websites that sell domain names. It is best to choose a domain name that's closely related to your business name. You can learn more on how to choose a domain name here.

- Selecting your business structure that will best suit your needs i.e. will you operate as a sole proprietor, partnership, LLC or even corporation?

- Getting your EIN (Employer Identification Number). This is absolutely necessary, even if you are running a business with zero employees.

- Obtaining your business permits/licenses. There are those who think running an online business excludes them from the realities of running a physical business. Well, they are wrong. The fact that the internet is your turf does not excuse your business from requiring sales tax or even home businesses licenses. Of course, a lot of this stuff is dependent on the state that you are in.

Note: The thing is; you can skip this step if you are still experimenting different business options to find what works for you before you can officially deal with the paperwork. However, if you have found one thing that works (remember we've already discussed how to choose a product and other important information), don't delay to fulfill the above.

If you were running a brick and mortar business and have dealt with all the above, then your brick and mortar business arm would now be free to go off and cover as much physical ground as you would deem necessary. If the business was in real estate for instance, you could immediately make the necessary steps to acquire real estate or some commercial space, which you could then flip for a tidy profit. This is ecommerce, however. You cannot simply start firing away.

As an ecommerce business owner, you will have to work on building your online presence before you can start to think of making profits.

Creating Your Site

Developing a website can seem almost impossible for a complete beginner. That's perhaps why hiring a website developer is a priority for many people venturing into ecommerce for the first time. Well, the good thing about hiring a professional is that you will get a unique professionally designed website, which will impress anyone visiting your website and definitely increase the number of sales/conversions. The only downside to hiring a website developer is the cost involved; it might cost you anywhere between $100-$500 to make a functional ecommerce website. You can hire an overseas developer on Upwork.com, Fiverr.com, Freelancer.com and many other marketplaces.

Note: Before your site goes live, it needs to be hosted; hosting costs around $10 a month. You can get it hosted on the site you purchased the domain from or choose another hosting provider depending on reputation. You can learn how to choose a hosting provider here.

Well, if you don't have a lot of money to spent to get started, you can as well create a website. Gone were the days when creating a website was only a thing for nerds. Different ecommerce companies have developed systems that any beginner can use to create a functional ecommerce store in minutes! Some use a seamless drag and drop mechanism, which any user can use to create a website. For instance, you can use Weebly website builder, Wix website builder, GoDaddy Website builder, Duda One Website builder, or Squarespace website builder. All these are easy to use thanks to their drag and drop capabilities.

If you want to be a good-looking website without having to spend too much money on web development, the best option is to use WordPress. All you need to do is to install it on your host (the site you purchase a domain from will probably have a WordPress install function; use that to install WordPress on your site). WordPress is easy to use, has lots of powerful capabilities and the platform has a vibrant community, which you can learn from. While WordPress is ordinarily a blogging platform, you can create an ecommerce store by installing the necessary plugins. Some of the popular plugins include WooCommerce, Magento and Shopify; simply search for these on WordPress.org or within your WP-Admin panel. You can learn the specifics on how to get started in the links below:

Wpbeginner.com

Shivarweb.com

The thing is; 'easy installation' is relative; you might still not get it even after reading how to set up a WordPress ecommerce store. What do you do? Well, if you are a complete WordPress beginner, you can hire someone on Fiverr.com, Upwork.com or Freelancer.com to set up your WordPress site; it will cost you about $30-$50 to get this done.

The beauty about using some of the systems/tools mentioned above is that they allow you to connect your website to payment processing systems like PayPal, which makes it easy for people to pay you for the products or services you have on sale. Through such payment systems, it becomes very easy to accept credit card payments from all over the world.

List Your Products

Once you have your website developed, the next logical step is to publish whatever it is you want to be selling. How do you go about it? Here are some ideas to keep in mind:

- ✓ Make sure you have high quality product images: Customers judge things by their images; if they cannot make out how a product really looks like, you can bet that they are unlikely to make a purchase. The thing is; if you are selling products by major brands, you are likely to have access to a wide array of high quality photos (the supplier will probably send you such photos), which means you won't have to worry about creating your own photos. But if you are making your own products, you have two options i.e. hire a professional product photographer to capture the products for you or do it yourself. If you want to go the DIY route, you must learn how to capture great photos. You can learn how about it here.

- ✓ Product descriptions will make or break your ecommerce business. If your product is not as described, you probably will have returns. Therefore, strive to have exceptionally crafted product descriptions. It is best to hire a copywriter to help you with this if you are not a writer. You can hire a copywriter on iWriter.com, Upwork.com, Freelancer.com, Writearticlesforme.com, TheWritingSummit.com, Epicwrite.com etc.

As a rule of thumb, make your site easy to use because the easier it is to get around your ecommerce store, the easier your customers will pay you without spending too much time trying to figure out how your website operates.

Let me explain this with an example of Roxanne King.

Back in the year 2011, Roxanne King, who was already a successful blogger started making and revising her own skin care products. She did this at her home. Her experimenting in skin care products was as a result of necessity- having had problems with preservative-heavy commercial skin care products and being several months pregnant, she thought she could do better. The products worked for her. But she wasn't selling them at the time. In fact, it was not until 2 years later, that she made the jump from giving other people her home-crafted cleansers as presents to selling them. She started selling them in farmer's markets before transitioning to selling them online.

This was how she began her own ecommerce site on her blog theholisticmama.com. Roxanne credits the simplistic structure of her site to attracting a large customer base within a relatively short time. All there was to it was a page I had on my blog in the beginning. I named that page 'Shop' and for the next few months, I sold just this one product," King says. "The page had a button for folks to make their payments with PayPal. I got this one by using PayPal's site and then copy-pasting it onto my blog. I feel the simplicity of it all was initially what drew in the customers, especially those housewives who felt a little sick every time they tried accessing sites only to be hit by color and other eccentricities that come with sites. I feel most of these people just want to come in and be able to purchase their product quickly before getting out of there. They have other things to do"

Tip: You will need a system for capturing emails for current and prospective customers if you want to keep them engaged throughout the pre-purchase and post purchase process. If you are using a WordPress site, all you need to do is to install the relevant plugins e.g. MailChimp, AWebber, Getaresponse, and others.

Once your site is fully set up with a list of the products you want to sell, the next step is to market it to generate sales. We will learn how to go about it next.

Where The Rubber Meets The Road: Marketing Your Ecommerce Store

The truth is; there are probably tens or even hundreds of ways through which you can attract people to your ecommerce store with some of the common ones including the following:

Social Media: Social media marketing is a wide subject. However, at its simplest, you can do the following particularly on Facebook; Set up a Facebook Page for your ecommerce store, share the page to your networks then hope that you will generate sales from that. Once you do that, the next bit is to be posting valuable information about the products you have on sale, as well as other valuable information that can add value to your audience e.g. creative ways to use various products, how to choose between different product categories, product testimonials, behind the scenes of your business etc. If you want to take it a bit further, you can post promoted posts to generate traffic to your page or to the particular post and ultimately generate sales. As I already stated, social media marketing is a wide subject, which we may not cover in this book. To help you in the process, you can learn more about it here, here and here.

SEO (Search Engine Optimization): If you want to literally make it huge online, you MUST leverage on the power of search engines in bringing high quality, relevant traffic to your ecommerce store. It doesn't matter whether your ecommerce store was originally developed to cater to a certain keyword; you must optimize your website for search engines to ensure your current and prospective customers find you. You don't want people not to find your website even when they are searching for the exact keyword. You can hire an SEO agency to optimize your website for search engines or you can do it yourself by following this comprehensive guide. You could even use paid advertising on Google AdWords if you have some money to spare.

Blog: I already stated that one of the ways of increasing awareness about your ecommerce store is to blog about it. Therefore, don't stop at just the basics. Keep blogging about it, share the content on various social networks and make it sharable (on your blog). You will be amazed at how people find it easy to buy products from someone they consider an authority or someone they trust.

Tip: *Blog…But Not On Your Own Blog*

The trouble with most ecommerce blogs is they are as boring. Most ecommerce bloggers only write because they read in some 3 page guide that they HAVE to blog on their products. As a result, very few people are actually too keen on browsing the ecommerce blogs available. How about you flip this dynamic, so that you get to benefit?

You can do anything, from hosting lots of guest posts featuring guests you feel have interesting stories to tell, to guest blogging on other people's blogs. This will work to draw people your way and ultimately, toward your ecommerce site.

To be extraordinary, you have to apply yourself in a way that is out of the ordinary. You could say that another word for extraordinary is "unconventional". You now have an idea on what you need to do to start an ecommerce business and market it just like everyone else. You know of the necessary tools to help you start your ecommerce business and you know what to do to ensure you remain on the path toward success.

But what can you do to speed up your success? Here are some unconventional, under-used avenues that you can employ for your own gain.

Use Reddit, And Use It As Aggressively As You Can

If you do not know what Reddit is, it is time you crawled out from under that rock you have been under. Reddit is often referred to as the front page of the internet. It is a huge social bookmarking site that caters to just about every interest in the world. The different interests and categories are divided into "subreddits". For instance, you can bet that there is a subreddit for that edgy TV show that you thought nobody else but yourself watched.

How does it work? Well, Reddit uses an upvote-downvote system, where the most upvoted items make their way to the top.

Reddit is basically one giant pool where people converge to share important stuff or just banter about. One of the best ways to use reddit is to hold an AMA (Ask Me Anything) session where the users will ask you questions on your item of expertise (in this case, you will be marketing your ecommerce products).

It is a brilliant way to market yourself, as you will be interacting with at least a couple of thousands of people at a time. Many businesspeople and artists are taking this route.

Podcasting Is Alright

The podcasting world is growing at quite some rate. What is even better is that the ecommerce world is yet to catch on, as far as podcasting goes. That's why if you move fast, you could easily make a killing.

People love to have a podcast with them to listen to perhaps because with podcasts, morning jogs and long drives are not the same.

There are multiple ways you can manipulate the podcast market. You can appear as a guest in podcasts that are relative to your products, and thus have a chance to market it. Or, you can throw caution to the heavens and start your own podcast program.

Provided you keep it regular and seek to have as many guests as you can, it will eventually pick up. The ecommerce world is yet to take podcasting with the seriousness that it deserves. If you are smart, you will embrace podcasting and keep it around.

Coupon Sites

Coupon sites, such as FatWallet and RetailMeNot, that document the existing coupon codes for several sites are usually a consumer's secret weapons. When buying an item online, most consumers promptly keyword-search the business and promo code so as to unearth existing coupon codes that they can use. When searching time comes, why not ensure that there is indeed something waiting?

Coupon sites are a great way to push a promotion that you're running, especially if you want to get rid of closeouts and old stock. Instead of burning precious advertisement dollars on such activities as promos, you may leverage these coupon sites to display these offers instead.

In addition, the coupon site RetailMeNot's users do love sharing codes. Thus, the more coupons that appear with superb offers, the more likely it is that the merchant shall rise to the site top. Merchants who do not allow for sharing generally experience drops in views and click throughs, and therefore little rise in sales.

With everything you have learnt in mind, I believe it would be great to learn from others who have gone before you. In the next chapter, we will have a summary of some of the experiences of other people in ecommerce; reading about their experiences will definitely help you to pick up something that will put you on the path to success.

How Do You Build An Ecommerce Business Where You Sell Your Own Product With Zero Money?

Note that we have already touched on how ecommerce sites work, when you are selling another person's products (products made by other people). Here, we will focus on starting your own ecommerce gig while selling your own product.

Many guides out there will pitch loads of "the most ideal way to build your ecommerce business" ideas, but very few of them will actually take you through the process using true, actionable accounts from people who have succeeded. This is not that kind of guide. In this chapter, you will be taken through the process of setting up a successful ecommerce business via the replies to questions, by an individual who is a novice just like you are (well, he is only a relative novice, since he has already managed to generate profits of up to $1,000). You will be able to see what prompted him to go into ecommerce. You will be able to see how his idea was birthed among other things.

If you are a rational human being, and you most likely are one seeing as you took the time to read this guide, you will use his simple model and process to inspire you to your own success. Oh, and you will not have to think too hard. This chapter will do a proper job of making the extrapolation by you, the reader, of the example here, as easy as possible. This chapter is a guide on how to build your ecommerce business with no money through the experiences of an ecommerce businessman who is not quite clear off the woods yet. But he is well on his way. Sometimes, the best lessons are to be learned from beginners like yourself and not experts, as you will be able to relate to their examples better.

The Example: Brian Pulliam of Backplane
(www.backplane.com)

What Led To You Starting Your Ecommerce Store?

I injured my back. Few people understand the importance of proper posture, until they injure their backs and go through the hell that is rehab. Like so many people, I made my daily bread by sitting on a chair all day long and doing office work. So, I decided to make a product that would ease my back issues when I was sitting in the office. I realized it was a massive help, and I immediately wanted to help others.

How Did You Determine That People Needed Your Product And Thus, Would Want To Buy It?

I went about this in a simple way. I simply asked people to buy before I had even made a single product. Pre-sales is a potent thing. Not only does it ensure that you will hit the ground running, but it drastically cuts financial risk. The other thing is I was confident in the effectiveness of my product, as it had worked wonders for me.

How Did You Create Your Product's First Version?

My product is all about posture. My PT and my chiropractor had suggested I use a foam-roll, laid along the spine. I conducted measurements on the degree my shoulders relaxed when I used the foam roll, and then I picked up my hacksaw and began experimenting. To put it simply, I failed a lot of times with my first prototype. In fact, so bad was my first prototype that it gave an early customer of mine a fierce migraine. It would have been quite easy to give up, but I was smart enough to realize that with repeated failure, the breakthrough gets closer and closer.

What Did You Learn From The Whole Process?

- Presales are key (see above)

- Failure is alright. Get rid of your fear for it.

- Focus on the fundamentals: Ask the people what problems they have, identify a remedy, pre-sell this remedy, over deliver, with your execution, make sure to be where customers are, and then show these customers how this remedy cures their problems.

What Challenges Did You Face?

Convincing people to buy at first was pretty hard. They love to see a testimonial or two and sometimes, they want something extra to convince them that they are making a good buy. Then you have that group of people that are skeptical because the product is not made of fancy material. I am the sort of guy who likes to keep it simple. The wallet suffers less too, if anything.

What Was Your Most Memorable Moment About Selling?

There are many things I could cite. But I think the process of practicing failure is right at the top. The process of failing repeatedly, both in my prototypes and in trying to pitch my product for sales was quite eye-opening. I remember watching the popular entrepreneur show "Shark Tank", after I had managed to successfully pre-sell my product. A lot of the time, I found myself yelling at the contestants. "What exactly do you mean that you are "pre-revenue"? Is that even a thing?"" What did you say your inventory was? Holy cow, how on earth will you sell that?"

Failure is not talked about enough. Only through practicing failure, will you overcome fear of failure.

What Have You Learned About Selling Physical Products?

I had to learn not to expect perfection at every turn. It was not a lesson I was ready to learn, but having to churn out prototype after prototype, to the count of 27, has a way of humbling a man and reminding him that he is an imperfect being who was born to make mistakes.

I'm easier to be around now, and I do not expect my products to be superhuman-perfect. I just try to give the best that I can to my customer and I recommend every other business owner to embrace this model. The other thing I have learned is to ignore people. I mean, fellows who I know will push me a level higher are always welcome. But you have this breed of people who think they are geniuses; who immediately shoot down your model and give you scaling advice even though they have never made a dollar in their lives from ecommerce. These fellows and their methods are best left to themselves.

What Advice Would You Give To Prospective Ecommerce Business Owners?

The most important piece of advice I can give to you is to get a customer base ASAP. This is not just so that you can have people to hand over their dollars to you once you have your product ready- every interaction you have with your customer base is important in ensuring you come up with the best product possible. Customers, especially potential customers, tend to have a lot of concerns. Cover the bases they bring to your attention so that you have a product that is tailored to best suit them before you even make a single sale. The other thing you should know is that with an ecommerce store, you will never have the problem of having "too many customers", as you would have if you were running a manual shift.

How Much Have You Made So Far?

I am up to 1000 dollars. Note that when I started out, I had an amount of zero dollars (and quite the vision in my head too).

If you follow his model of identifying a problem within the community, addressing this problem by coming up with a suitable remedy and then crafting your product so that you can enrich the community as a whole, it will only be a matter of time before you are successful as an ecommerce business owner.

Conclusion

The Ecommerce world is not an easy one to penetrate and master. It is also not a hard one to establish oneself in. You just have to play the game in a smart manner. It is important to gain as much knowledge as possible. Try and be unique. Do not be so broad that you have problems standing out in a saturated market. Also, you should remember that no product is beneath you; there are people making a killing buying and selling products that are worth less than $5.

Thank you again for downloading this book!

I hope this book was able to help you to understand how to make money through ecommerce.

The next step is to implement what you have learnt.

Finally, if you enjoyed this book, would you be kind enough to leave a review for this book on Amazon?

Click here to leave a review for this book on Amazon!

Thank you and good luck!

Made in United States
North Haven, CT
14 May 2023

36553668R00024